steeplechase

pitt poetry series

nancy krygowski and jeffrey mcdaniel, editors

steeplechase

angela ball

university of pittsburgh press

Published by the University of Pittsburgh Press, Pittsburgh, Pa., 15260

Manufactured in the United States of America
Printed on acid-free paper
10 9 8 7 6 5 4 3 2 1

ISBN 13: 978-0-8229-6765-1
ISBN 10: 0-8229-6765-0

Cover art by aremihc on AdobeStock.com
Cover design by Melissa Dias-Mandoly

Publisher: University of Pittsburgh Press, 7500 Thomas Blvd., 4th floor, Pittsburgh, PA 15260, United States, www.upittpress.org
EU Authorized Representative: Easy Access System Europe, Mustamäe tee 50, 10621 Tallinn, Estonia, gpsr.requests@easproject.com

For Mike Magee, 1955–2024

contents

I.

2.

3.

steeplechase

I.

Hares

Not mine but I'll take some—
not too much,
just part. Not the best part—
It could be best, though,
no way
of knowing, I'll take
just the blue part,
the part that includes
a cantilever bridge,
or maybe the brown part, that includes
a horse's halter, I'll take the part
that is cream and gray, like the mushroom
in my path, maybe the roughed-up
part, teeth marks on it,
dragged from a dank cellar,
the part that has deliquesced,
the part just painted
to resemble a mouse, the part vaccinated
by flood, the part
that has rubbed
against roses. The part with dropsy. The part
that flusters some; that flusters no one.
The part that brandishes endorphins,
the part that returned to life, sorely
inconveniencing the staff, the part that knows
whereof it speaks, the part that waits longest
with no coffee, no chips, no cigarettes, the part

that locks my gaze, asks my pity,
rests close against me,
watches with me as two hares begin boxing
in the solemnity of dawn.

James

I made a clay sculpture
He had broad shoulders
and slim hips   I was working on
what Rilke calls "the center
of procreation" when James offered
his help   *If you'd like I can do*
that part   I was galvanized
Powerless to stop   The slip felt
cool eager   I thought of Camille
Claudel and her courage
But it was loneliness
that bent me to the task
I should confess that the statue
was tiny its broad shoulders
about one and one-half inches
wide I once knew someone who made
tiny horses from straw He gave me one
to give someone else
That person died   I kept the horse
My house ate it   as it has eaten
James   I imagine finding him
astride the tiny horse

Half-Sister Who Floated Out to Sea

A calm day; a few boats
on the water, sails jaunty

as a dandy's pocket square.
In the distance, one cumulus.

Nearer, the promontory
of an island, its bristling crown.

A dog sniffing the shoreline resembled "Tige,"
who used to sell Buster Brown shoes.

The tide spread itself like a delicate shawl.
Every night, in my sleep, my older half-sister

tried to live with me. She thought I would
introduce her to people, men
in particular. Every night

she was bitter, disappointed. I failed
to bring her anything she wanted,
though I asked a man, while fondling him,
did he have friends;

and, what's more, seldom asked her to sleep
in her own room with her paintings,
their redolent wet oils.

For my part, I hoped to find generous
friends I could emulate, learn from;

I looked everywhere there was. Found
a cemetery's obelisk; a fire station's
row of high boots.
                                        Meanwhile,
my half-sister held one corner

of my blouse, the one she had declared
a great color for me. Cotton
voile. I love the word "voile"; I pull it
close.

At Dairy Queen, I ordered for her;
the "Monkey Tail," since her lips wouldn't say it.

Under the sky, the same pine tops, shape
cut by pinking shears.

I take note of days: the one for the number Pi;
various eating contests; eclipses, complete
and partial; the time and place for disposal
of white goods.

How long since she went floating? Long.
I pull on time like clear tape; I reach cardboard;
a new roll begins.

I See You Everywhere

If I could I would also see math
the radial increments of petals   the fractals

of the coast
that if measured correctly
would be the length of heaven

If I could I would open a business
in smiling   We would always be
in the red

Along with you I love
the self-described housewife
In my first composition class

who spent an essay
praising straight teeth

Along with you and with her I love Nils Bohr
who said at the very end

of his first essay *And now I would like to mention*
aluminum

No matter how much you love someone
you must forget them sometimes
to avoid madness   to let it happen

I found out on TV

you can take two men's ties
and make an obi sash
from them   can you take two men
and make a sports car out of them
that will shift standard or automatic
to match your inclination

from two towels you can make
a unisex apron   can you make
a pansexual towel that travels the world
caressing everyone
from two towels can you make
a body of water that takes us along
to a deluxe park of candy cigarettes
a bathing hut lined with fake fur
and scraps of letters from two people
still destined to meet

The Termites' Violins

You stay in back of the night
if there's no room in the front
The back is where
the books with fade-prone paper
go   the tubas with the wrong twist
the termites' violins   the rubies made of paste
that joins wet to dry
old-style flashbulbs that shoot
then fall   breaking underfoot
like extra zeroes   the gray violence
of early cartoon mice
The front of the night
is where all the affection goes
the hair mussing the rough housing
the play kisses that are real

A Confluence at Paducah

Driving across a bridge
then another then another
where rivers join
and split off   we glimpsed current
lit by dawn or shadowed by branches
It occurs to me   how many hours
were spent drawing plans
calculating loads   graphing corrosion
erosion of banks   silt ratios
pliability of mud
strength of basins   How often
late at night the draughtsman
leaned on a pencil

All for two people
to enter and leave
a handful of states
bewilderment confusion oneness

Freak Storm

Snow   you must be afraid
you settle   so carefully
you must not remember
the winters you spent
with me   up north
my wooden sled
that had a kind of rudder
mounted in front
so my mittened hands
could turn it   evading
a rock   a fallen branch
as I lay on my stomach
with other children
as we sped headfirst
down a long rise
of whiteness
feeling you fall

Golden Dragon

In an airport waiting room   a woman said
to me   *You don't have to smile all the time*
you know

Another woman said to her lover
of my behavior towards
my husband   *She defers*

My childhood home was anger
passive aggression or fists or both
What would happen was
up in the air   where I wished
to go

A smile is camouflage.
Deference   cheap insurance
In the case above
the cost was eating
a Chinese meal
when I was not hungry

These days hunger is my sole business
The Golden Dragon stays far off
breathing its fire where it pleases

Steeplechase

Steeples have a big
responsibility, upholding
the faith.

In a country of churches
I do a running
study of steeples: their

gradients, stages, angles
of ascent, presence
or absence of terminal
cross.

All are white,
though a few have begun
to discolor with rust
or rot; to lean, vaguely
lapsed.

None have belfries, those noisy
papist extravagances.
Only height
asserts itself, slimming
toward the infinite.

One has a lightning rod
that might be blasphemous.

Today, for the first time,
a steeple with windows
on all sides. Miniature panes with white
dividers radiating sunrise.
Who could get in
to look out? Maybe a person's head
could, rising from an attic
ladder. I would love to see
the face of someone
so alone.

Unsent Love Letters

Dear Charles De Gaulle
I love you but your hat
is not very flattering

Dear Mr. Lincoln
Your wife
is too short for you

Dear Alan Rickman
When I saw you sitting alone
in the Italian restaurant
I should have leapt on you
It would have been
worth a try

Dear George Gordon Lord Byron
My hopeless affection for you
is causing me to drink too much
Luckily I have your hangover recipe
Hock and soda water

Dear Percy Bysshe Shelly
Your ideas about free love
work much better for men
than for women I challenge you
Go ahead
Prove me wrong

Incomparable Coffee Shop

Hospitals appear
in small groups   suddenly
as if released from above
by sterile claws

They boast many
lightning rods   bare needles
poking upward

to prevent
immolation

Inside
the Insistence of white
its clarity
color of exile

infiltrates the hair
of sufferers
Expressions age ten years
in an afternoon

Consider the one man
ever to drive to the hospital expressly
to lunch at their coffee shop

He liked the chili
"Of course it's from a can" his wife
scoffed   But going there
voluntarily is a privilege

sure to make
meat beans sauce
extraordinary   just as any evening

can transform by dressing up
for the hell of it

drawing our admiration
to the fabulous   catastrophic drag show
of a sunset
made of dust

Dirt Road Near Harrisville

Here's a partial fence
whose wood
resembles a lost dog
with stiff gray fur

A pile of fill dirt
recalls a mountain
the woman climbed as a girl

with a strange boy whose
long expressive fingers
grazed her cheek

A water tower
the badge

not needing to be shown
in *The Treasure of The Sierra Madre*

A bunched-up undershirt
the twentieth century

How constant
the presence of mourning

These goldenrod heads
drooping together
the women of Thebes.

Gym Suit

My thighs ballooned from its
one brief piece
my broad back strained
its buttons
The class had a system
We lined up in teams
Each had a captain a popular girl
Are you regular our captain
asked   meaning period
Yes I always said   *O Captain*
my Captain thin and quick
blonde of hair slim of hips

My Captain O my Captain
so as to skip the shower
Its slick of minor devils
thin and quick   *my Captain*
sleek of hair
kicked the gym teacher
my Captain was practicing balance beam
the gym teacher spotting
My Captain O my Captain
The gym teacher entered a coma
The gym teacher is in hell   I call
to *her come out of there*
now
I have one thing
I want to say

Tulipmania

Where did they go the men
of yesteryear they are snowy
now then they were inappropriate
unavailable interested in a boff
or two or in concealing impotence
of various kinds
none of which could
discourage me
in the slightest Still in love
I content myself
with imagining the flourishes
our two pianos
could have traded It's something like
the tulip frenzy in The Netherlands Four demented years
in which the Semper Augustus
with its proud variegated red
beggared expense Like the Netherlanders
who failed to obtain it I comfort myself
with a framed likeness
placed just right to observe
each morning upon waking
to rehearse to speculate

I've Never Fled from a Stolen Vehicle

though I have fled from a life
and just now from a sick room
full of a police reality show

to walk down a road with drainage ditches
on each side   Everything needs drainage
people animals houses

Ahead there's a large motionless cat
thank God alive and glaring my way
as I pass   My sweetheart has

a stoma for drainage
Also a port   where no ships arrive

This road could be called ugly
Who's to say that a splash
of silver gravel
Isn't beautiful   and the little cliffs above
the ditches

Eating People Is Wrong

Says this title
but it's circumstantial
When people eat people
it is usually for very good reason
as when a dog eats a shoe
to keep its owner close

When people eat people
personal space is violated
a boundary dissolves

as when angels fight with
or impregnate people
under circumscribed
conditions

the body is abundantly surprised
to find elements so like itself
travelling through it
making no comment whatsoever

The alimentary canal
sans gondoliers
is as long as a crumpled
coastline   One may sail there
secure   minus fear of pirates
cared for by
the truest of hosts

Confession

I was eight maybe
There was a large can
a wisp of smoke emerging
delicate as fog
My hands went in
and came out with something   Wood?
Cardboard? I knew friction
made fire   I rubbed the pieces
and sure enough there was the warm thought
of fire then fire
A flame I dropped
that followed itself across grass
it was a wide conversation
it seemed very free
unconcerned   happy to play
with vacancy
The Fire Department arrived
with big disapproval but I was gone
I am still gone

Two Trees

In memory of Adam Zagajewski

I am drinking a tree. Not exactly.
Not as exactly as the branches
lay, self-sectioned, over the round space
they had shaded, till workers
piled them at the curb. Not as exactly
as I planted it, seventeen years
past. A fig. The map
of its leaf. Before leaving
last summer, I gathered
some fruit, froze it. Left much,
a last harvest, disrespected.
My breakfast this morning
was figs, blended with other fruits,
and the phone image of a tree
my friend said his great friend
had loved. That is, what is left of it:
inexact taxonomy, sticks
on a brow of ground.

2.

In Walt Whitman's Great Poem

lilacs bloom'd in every dooryard
A train passed
flag draped
huffing station to station
while men removed their stovepipe
hats and women confined
by the bones of a sea mammal
pressed lace handkerchiefs
to the corners of their streaming
translucent eyes   All was still
for President Lincoln and death
No one burst from the dooryard in anger
over some perceived slight
or to announce that supper was ready
No woman removed her hoop
and pantaloons for her husband
to array himself atop her

Abraham Lincoln was partly great
and partly ordinary   He is ordinary
on the nights he visits his
memorial   a lilac in his lapel
stares in wonderment
at his beard of stone
grown on the advice
of a small girl

What Better Way to Meet Someone Than to Fall in Love

It is good to meet someone
when your mind is floating

You have removed your glasses
and these people are very young

Does education affect one's ability
to fall in love

Is handedness involved
Trust as in diving or numismatics

Famous people dislike talking to strangers
of love   That's why I am

not famous but strange   I ask the person waving me on
over a torn highway   Are you in love

I go to the courthouse to ask the judge
to the hospital to ask the obstetrician

to the morgue to ask the pathologist
I am full of questions but not a test

so much as a result   Is it an achievement
to love   Is morning as happy about love

as night is   When a physicist discovers something
infinite   that's love but not as much

as when you hear their step
smell their scent   remember

What does love share with science
Belief in the ignored detail   Belief
that no knowledge is permanent
or impossible

Cloud Society

It used to be
people put their cars in neutral

and coasted downhill
through coteries

of gnats   past pulses of fireflies
here   *no here*   *no over here*

like the visual field tests
required to chart the narrowing

Once I knew an actress whose hair
swung   pale

against her chin   Also an actor
with generous features

I liked the familiarity of
backstage   space
raw and scattered

You think of rejoining a conversation
but then

that's out
of the question

and what's in the question
is days of reading   writing

a report for the Cloud Society
A drive that's shadows on a film strip
and I think of my actor friend

how the cinder glows and subsides
as he smokes   leans
against a   remnant
of the city wall

Have you heard the one where

a man cuts down a bunch of trees
by mistake then tries to reattach them
to their stumps with duct tape
have you heard the one where the raw food
nut tries to cook in reverse
I will have you know that the Himalayas
are still rising   the plates under them
still pushing against each other
like children in a bouncy house
most mountains are too old for me
but not those   I would like to summit one
to personally say hi   to all the satellites
travelling backwards in time
with so many handsome and beautiful faces

Spokes

Are you tense with grief
though once a spillage
of happy thoughts
Could there be a cistern for the mind
a filter of healthy stones
Whatever happens focus on Parma
the moment of the fizzy wine
charcuterie   fried bread
the moment of handholding
just as the new and beautiful
Madonna passes on the shoulders
of the handsome   the strong
followed by those on crutches   in
wheelchairs with paper birds
attached to their spokes

I Wander the Hotel Where I Had a Romantic Adventure

Many think I am employed here

I pause to dust a plant

or seize a piece of lint

from a rug   Hold aloft

a glass of water

to regard it with

a critical eye   To be honest

I am lost in the atrium

the forecourt the anteroom the mezzanine

No one to scout my doubtful progress

through the self-consciousness

of halls   metallic and plush

the ruined villages of breakfast trays

The passing sky

a supernumerary

scarcely felt by the shear walls

beginning in bedrock

to support their live and dead loads

Dirty Versions of Famous Rounds

I'm sorry   I can't remember them   but if you just substitute
underpants   for most of the nouns
you will get the idea
For many a first taste
not of sex but cynicism
and its easy one-upmanship
When kids sung them I wanted to run away
In fact I want to run away now
Despite loving Baudelaire and *Flowers of Evil*
I don't want what used to be called
stews   where people simmered all day all night
in their passions   I don't want   *Let's do it in the road*
I am in tune with the male bowerbird in Papua
who builds a showplace from wreathed twigs and shiny pull tabs
on the thinnest speculation that it   might   perhaps   attract
a mate

A ghost brought her castle

as plus-one An elaborate cornice

framed her transparent head
Her dress was all drapery

and pull ropes *This is a strange party*
she said

This is no party I said I was trying to reconcile
the plebian with the royal

up with down and crosswise attraction and repulsion
to the earthy to the elegant

You are a fool she said *The tillers of soil*
have turned into so-called peasant loaves

We aristocrats are still ourselves Reinforced
by precious metals by velvet by pearls

Look at this article in the Ghost News
She held out a transparent paper its front page

announcing the activities of the glittering deceased
We support orphan ghosts ghosts on the spectrum

ghosts with aphasia fugue state cancer lumbago . . . .

I Like the Word "Bedchamber"

it makes the bed

most essential

chambered

like a bullet

Mr White and Mrs Green

You look at a flower and wonder
Is it too early like last year's
blueberries
becoming phantoms
Like actors whose scripts have been stolen
plants don't know when
to enter

Among the true charges
leveled by a long-ago friend
You came early
to your surprise party

I imagined
that being somewhere
makes you belong

My knowledge of human nature
was the automatic rightness
of a print family
who taught me reading
from a world where last names
were colors and occupations
permanent I'm still on the page
where Spot gets a bone and Dick and Jane
arrive at their grandparents' farm
The barn is dark red
All of day is one place

There were cities in our eyes

How did they get there   By narrowing
to a point   Foreshortened

metropolises spun around themselves
light narrowing to dark
dark to light their pivots
sometimes a park
sometimes a wine glass
full of pity or a loaf
made of bad jokes

There were cities in our eyes
How could we see each other
full of the wrong demographic
cranes and earth movers interested only
in chugging back and forth
wreathed in sallow dust

We were like games after rats had eaten
the faces from cards and the pips
from the dice

Some of us held slot machines
inside   Some of us photocopiers
Some of us plats

We were a chord
Not yet in existence
We were a diminishing fifth

We went along stealing algorithms
Went along stealing addresses
The cities were angular
They levitated
and fell

We had ice cubes inside us
and a pleasant rain smell
associated with woods

Lake Forgetful

I live where this lake lives
cupped atop ground water's table
for all to take in   I talk about water
because we're made of it
though it's disorienting to think so
There is the forgetting water
There is the remembering water
The water dyed yellow from coal byproducts
The water that tumbles gold
deep in its meshes   The water that leaves its shadow
for sunlight to dry   The water made to seem
as if running uphill (this
a vile trick)   The water that stops for confab
The water that when cold enough
becomes edible stone   The water that writes in longhand
words not meant to be read

Man-Chaser

I have always been known
for chasing men. I chase them
over historic bridges and through
the halls of distinguished
institutions   I borrow techniques
from pursuers of rock stars
who sometimes want to be caught
My men don't   to elude me
one became an astronaut   another
a diver   several   I suspect   blended in
among the chess players
forever inviting challengers
near the decrepit city gates.
A friend took me aside *These men want*
someone THEY can chase   It's
in their blood   But like someone
going in for an ill-advised kiss
it is too late to change
my mission   Few comprehend.
the bond between
pursuer and pursued
how tight   how delicate

Small Wood Table with Attached Bench

Picnic of nothing for one! But
it's behind a chained gate with a bold
No Trespassing

where purple flowers, yellow flowers
have arranged
October's light

When I stare at it
I could swear

it means something

Its owner must know

one can't help but long
for a thing so mute

Amazing Accident

I have jettisoned the stages

that propelled me   the mirror stage the gruesome-face stage

the parrot stage

Replete with learning

I walk through low sky that is all around

though we prefer to imagine it

distant so as to see its colors

that multiply via fascinating overlay

The context I prefer for math is the physical world

Milk multiplied by itself equals cheese

that amazing accident that happens on cue

Dust multiplied by itself equals

a planet   I have heard that Mr. Edison

got his idea for records

from planetary rings   I have heard that Mr. Otis

got his idea for an elevator

from a treehouse   I have heard that Mr. Ferris

got his idea for a wheel from a south-sea islander's

spinning torches

Though I am loathe to think so

I have a feeling you are loathe to believe me

In fact it shatters my heart

In the same place it always shatters

which is good because bits of glue remain

beading the jagged edge

Protracted Engagement

I am trying to figure out why
once my grandparents had met at the famous Exposition
where a madman shot President McKinley
it took seven years
for Grandma to say yes
Mamie lived ten miles distant
from John   near the unfortunately named
town of Beaver   She was schoolmarm
the only kind of "marm"   rode to work
on a pony named Laura   sidesaddle
preserving decorum   Maybe it was that John
visited her parents' parlor on Sundays
via horse and buggy   a ten-mile trip
that took so long in winter
he could only stay for a cup of tea
to get home before dark
and play his mandolin to himself
while by lamplight   Mamie prepared again
to teach *Paradise Lost*   school was harder then
In Milton's great poem
marriage is a mixed bag
but there *are*
the beautiful lines
about supplying one another's defects
These might have done the trick   or maybe a moment
of dawn while Mamie saddled Laura

in which the mare named Pris
nudged her new foal to scramble up
from wet straw   find the teat   drink

We Have Heard of the Eyes of Texas

What about the eyes

of the low buildings

with their beds and coverlets

the forms whose position

must be changed manually

at appointed hours

The eyes that assure

that sham foods

shimmer with perfection

as they drop

from their conveyors

The eyes staring from parapets

at the milling prisoners' one hour

of daylight

Have you seen the piece of bark

Cristobal Columbus touted

as cinnamon

sure of his renaming

The people called Neolithic

sometimes had fire kits: a curved leaf
or simple wooden box containing
the elements   sticks that could be twirled
for friction   a flint to strike sparks
a coal that might be
re-ignited   to put cold
at arms' length   to cook a tuber
wakened from its underground bed
where it siphoned water from a tree
in secret
I burn to be the idea of fire
that the sticks   the flint   the coal
pull from its hiding place
in plain sight

Networking

Everyone will be at the convention
including several people I might have met
at the last convention
Who are they

My cohort of oldsters
 is exceptional
and insistent   favors scarves
and is excellent at useful bags
and judging distances
between the exhibits

I once met a lover here
It was the day after two
of my teeth fell apart
at a party   though I tried

hiding the remnants
the woman I had been talking with
quickly moved away

My convention lover assumed I was crazy
about sex but that wasn't
the case   It was touch
deprivation

Before today's convention
he let me know he was in a serious
affair and couldn't see me   There he is   walking
with his serious lover   who has long braids
and a green backpack

From outside the hotel comes the sound
of a pile driver   a rhythmic crash
like the pulse of a giant

Chit

I choose another century
in which I write with a quill
but don't like its boney point
and I move forward in time
to a grease pencil   I think of Liz Taylor
writing on a hotel mirror in angry lipstick
in *Butterfield 8*   in the days
when phone exchanges had names
and every switchboard was staffed by women
with the power to confound one utterance
with another   and there lived a waitress
who had utilized
the same pad and pencil for fifty years
who bought replacements
at Woolworth's on her brief
lunch hour and had never once carried home
the canary that sang bravely from the store's far reaches
Sang as if recognizing the waitress
as a bird who like it endured hardship so that others
might understand not to follow   not
to be caught forever in some toxic
enterprise   Suddenly I am her
A waitress who one day discovers
that I was long ago plucked
by a studio scout and am playing my greatest role
that of hash-slinger whose handwriting is stabbed
repeatedly by a chit spike
filled to the tip with short orders

No Island a Woman

I can't speak of him
any more than an island
can speak of a vessel
wrecked against it
captain and passengers
peopling swirls of currents
till they wash up
as torn missives
for oceanside towns
pushing taffy
and toy boats

3.

James Wright I Am Calling

on the special phone for the dead
You saved me with your poem
"Two Hangovers" though at the time
I had never had one Only a lingering belief
in misery I read you while my parents
slept in their separate rooms
their rage for each other
a flickering pilot light
I never met you It was said
you were a bad father
to your son another poet
I don't care
"Two Hangovers" was so friendly
It didn't care that I lacked friends
that I might never have one
that I walked forward looking down
possibly on a permanent basis

The Year of Uncancelled Flights

Planes kept taking off   flew to their destinations
The people in them had made sound decisions
Some of the planes were only   flying to be flying
There is so much in our lives
that doesn't fly
All airports are proud   they own a slice of sky
inscribe it with their planes' daily
nightly emissions   contrails displacing
the comitatus of clouds   Think of the decades
spent honing the wood
perfecting the angles   forging the propellers
Not invented for war   airplanes became war
Think of the monstrous engines of grief
We too are made for beauty and look
what happens

Man on the Street

The sentiments here expressed
belong not to me but to coffee
from other worlds
Belong
to the man on the street
eating the found stub
of a hotdog
in gasping bites   Belong
to the schoolboy
embarrassed by our association
though it existed only in a note
disavowing his interest in me
they belong to the feet I then wore
like sad destroyers
on an impeccable ocean
In case I have not said it
the sentiments here expressed
belong not to me but to my friend
who recently had to tell his step-
grandson that kicks are not needed
to establish Granddad's solid
presence   belong not to me
but to a former lover
I had longed to meet in the gleaming bath
of a posh hotel
now defunct.

Why I Love Going North

It connects you to The North Pole
the way doing something slightly crazy
connects you with craziness

the way sewing on a button
connects you with Balenciaga

and moving your feet
connects you with Usain Bolt

I am short on trajectories
long on stillness

I am trying to locate
a discus I threw
at an early age   the net
my volley cleared
in adolescence

Often it seems I'm balancing again
on the running board of a Chevy
while a now-late sister
learns to drive

Staring in disappointment
at a snapshot that turned my dog
into a distant lump

In bewilderment at cutouts of eyebrows
like torn-apart wings

In grief at a rectangle
where a woman and man hold each other
in a fast slow dance

I'm jigging around
full of music
in a honky-tonk burnt
by time   unlicensed
for dancing   thinking

let me   be a wet floor with a green gem
of bottle glass

a forest in rut with humus
from sweeps of broken trees

Path of Desire

Not above but
under duress

I sold a Contemporary
where I slept among Oaks

American Robins hid
behind

in play   I sold a wild Irish
boy   or was he

a Scot   gratis   before
he could finish

selling me   I sold

my promissory locket
my adverse possessions

the path of desire
once re-made

each morning

to a field of piebald
Shetlands In exchange

no one held out
to me

a disused trapeze   a net
with a woman-sized tear

a Little Blue Heron's

lake-edge side-eye

the spot where a car
shot from the highway

its cross
the straw fedora tacked
just above its arms

I Was Born in a Different Country

People were always stealing things
donuts light fixtures horses

who walked around with paint
dripping off of them

unsure where to belong
Burying stuff was not an option

Loose dirt gave it away
Someone stole my mother's hair

as it lay on her pillow
during an afternoon nap

A pond stole my sister's coupe
by attracting it in

Books weren't immune
Babar the elephant was taken

And at the end of *Anna Karenina* we found
only her fur muff
glistening with blood

He Is Karst Topography

Should he put foot wrong
he will fall through
himself
his string of naps
consortium of pills   his pet
a tiny lizard stuck to the window
gives pleasure   eats bugs
cannot eat mice
the price of an ad hoc room
former garage
Cars doze in the meadow
like creatures   His body
too full   grows its dark spaces
without consent
All is confused   Treatment burned away
fingerprints   Who is he

A Hard Cash Sky You Can Touch

For Steve Yarbrough

In the Mississippi delta
clouds are ample and beautiful
part of a large No Comment
that covers flats of fields
giant irrigation arms that inch
forward too slowly for detection
There are no detectives
here because crime is simply
in the air and there's no telling
how it can expiate itself if ever
Wrongs are buried   below stone
vases   peony stems sprung
petals gray   There's a long road
of pecan trees children once climbed
to get a good look   but they have gone
A football field   proud
and empty   made of pick-up
sticks   It has been raining
it has always been raining
One silo so dark
it must have won midnight
in a poker game
and Charley Patton's grave
scattered with guitar picks cheap pieces
of plastic that mean silence
is being played

The Most Fun

was driving a buckboard
drawn by a pony   Bonnie
piebald with wild transparent
eyes   I was with the Eliot twins
girls my mother didn't like   They grabbed
handfuls of pencils from her business desk
anyway   the buckboard tipped over
hurting no one but ending fun
forever   The Elliott twins were bossy
Later I would marry someone bossy
and rationalize that   too
The girl I was is still in me   She is hopeful
in her small space
close to the bone

Due to the Absence of a Mouth Moths Are Unable to Eat

It's good to write
where one is not supposed to
like in a salon to note
the ordinary debasement
of the word from meaning a place
where Marcel Proust and select friends
exchanged music
to one with flowery aerosols
and emphatic tattoos
Looking back as Proust did one recognizes
the flaws in happiness
that might
have sustained it
like ice sustains the corpses of mountaineers
helpless but determined
like an acid or mordant
cuts a metal surface to create
a design in intaglio
like water wakes a pan of blue pigment
so it may migrate to a subject's face
and flash it with sadness
like a caterpillar consumes a tapestry
before losing her mouth to become a Luna moth
of surpassing beauty
with one week to finish mating
and laying eggs so that she may press
against a window screen
the tragedy of her celadon wings

An Atmospheric River

heads to the west coast of the United States
Like a restless person it rolls over many times
It cannot tell you the towns it shadows
the quaint water towers that boys write on
in support of anarchy
the earthly rivers it must find too talkative
too blatant   The ground is not its department
It cannot tell you why it exists why
it travels from the equator
That kind of question
swells it with despair

A Dish of March

Old ghost I judge an oven's heat
by paper light yellow
light brown dark brown
Bake vegetables
beneath a sheet of water
for the time
it takes an adult
to walk two leagues
till an aroma rises to entice
an invalid from bed
I have no fixed kitchen
wear no toque
volunteer like a lane's
grassy spine
rifled by impetuous carriages
I was the first wife of Celsius
the second wife of Fahrenheit
Mercurial carmine thread
spector I glide
between boiling and freezing
the hectic and the breathless

He Abandoned Opinions

Commanded himself
to leave the sovereign state
of life   Left behind
all roadways   all the discarded hounds
loping alongside them
car washes   matter of fact and rubbery
with their catalogued scents
fast food kitchens' metallic grease
smug haberdasheries
ice cream shops   archives
performers in breakaway gowns   waiters
in mufti   aquariums of flower-like fish
relying on pumped-in air
the movie   *Imitation of Life*
in which a young woman must renounce her parentage
to live as the opposing race   Do advantages apply
when coupled with self-consciousness   fear
In choosing death did you renounce   birth
How are you   Are you having a hard time   what is going on
with you they asked   but by then you had left your body
behind   just a short time to return
reclaim   discard

Curiosity

I have a mirror that reflects only bulls
I think that Ferdinand would like it
but how to find him   He is a piece
of paper

I wander the halls of paper
wearing a red shirt
I see only my sister Olive Oyl
Tell me Sister   she asks
can I ever be glamorous
That question is above
my pay grade   I say

What's better is the marvelous way
you stretch your arms   so much more versatile
than Popeye's   his biceps only cans
with pasted-on pictures
of spinach

It Seems Every City

must have special access
to the sky   an aerial contrivance
that revolves at different speeds
from earth
Tourists   supreme   empowered
take in all neighborhoods at once
overlaid with worries about a dying parent
or friend   what the house sitters
might get up to
It isn't good to go up alone
descend to an empty room
take a book's advice
about dinner
Better to rendezvous with a friend
who identifies all statues   guides us to a boite
where we sip fizzy wine   eat mussels steamed in garlic
discuss the people   if any   we live with
When we are at home   I'll be discrete   say nothing
of our infinite smallness   the largess I grew to know

Days of Hunger

I have committed every fallacy
in the book   and more
Our finery feels sorry for us
Small blue flowers stay
close to the ground to avoid
damage   My stomach misses
your stomach   Even if I were an army
I could never travel on mine
it is delicate as a stamen
That man arrested in airport security
for carrying a hatchet
was really me
I once was a measuring stick
for a river   An arc lamp
in the House of Wax
In its days of hunger Cuba was me
Never to be released from its secret prison

World Land

Don't expect anything
says the house
Blankness gets more blank
Quiet more quiet
I am here to do
nothing   I can't decide
if you are here
or not and if so do you wonder
about the Venetian blinds
are they from Venice
Maybe that city washed over us
and left them behind
Once fortune seemed to
set me apart   Now misfortune
proves my importance   There is an ad
in the paper   A subdivision
wants more houses   It is called
World Land   A name both
vainglorious and humble
Would you move there with me
dear ghost since I have asked nicely
It has been discovered that chairs
communicate through a thrumming
whose pitch depends on their size
My love please translate if you can
what they are saying

acknowledgments

Many thanks to the editors of the following publications, where earlier versions of some of these poems appeared:

> *Birmingham Poetry Review*: "The Half-Sister Who Floated Out to Sea" (winner of the Collins Award), also published on *Verse Daily*; *Columbia Review*: "Small Wood Table with Attached Bench," "Steeplechase"; *Conduit*: "I Found Out on TV," "Freak Storm," "Have you heard the one where"; *Paris Review*: "Hares"; *Poetry Daily*: "Hares"; *Poetry Magazine*: "Two Trees"; *Three-Penny Review*: "I Was Born in a Different Country."

Thanks to the University of Southern Mississippi for granting me a sabbatical for fall 2023. Much appreciation is owed to dear and steadfast friends Theresa and Tony Hallgarten for welcoming me to their houses in France and England during that time, and thanks in particular to Theresa, a brilliant artist, for acquainting me with the Cloud Society and the term from landscape architecture, "Path of Desire," and for numerous other inspirations. Thanks to Dara Barrois/Dixon, Julia Johnson, and Donald Revell for their friendship and belief in my work. Much gratitude to Steve Yarbrough for being my best and most generative first reader.